Pearls for Breakfast
A 12-day devotional for women

Lynn Lewis

Text copyright © 2024 Lynn Lewis

The right of Lynn Lewis to be identified as the author of this work has been asserted by her in accordance with the Copyright, Designs, and Patents Act 1988.

All rights reserved.

No part of this publication may be reproduced or transmitted in any form or by any means, electronic or mechanical, including photocopy, recording or any information storage and retrieval system, without permission in writing from the author.

Independently published.

For permission requests contact Lynn Lewis at lynn.lewis24@hotmail.com

First edition: 2024

Scripture quotations are from The ESV® Bible (The Holy Bible, English Standard Version®), © 2001 by Crossway, a publishing ministry of Good News Publishers. Used by permission. All rights reserved.

ISBN: 9798334293465

All proceeds from the sale of this book will go to LIV Durban.

Anna
This is for you, Chickadee!

Contents

Introduction	1
Elizabeth	5
Anna	9
Martha	11
The Freed Woman	13
The Healed Woman	15
The Well Woman	19
Mary, Martha's Sister	23
The Woman Who Worshipped	25
The Women Disciples	27
The Forgiven Woman	29
Mary Magdalene	31
Mary, The Mother of Jesus	35

Introduction

I have spent the last thirty years leading women's ministry. As life changed, so did the ministry. The privilege of teaching and encouraging women to go deeper with Jesus, to live in the Presence of God, and to build the kingdom of God, has been immense. It's my jam, and it's living life in the sweet spot. Thank You, Jesus, for allowing me to do this.

It seemed obvious then, that if I was going to publish anything, it would be to cheer women on, to challenge women, and to encourage women to chew on the scriptures about women. I love how Jesus championed women! I love that He still champions women today! I love that He is a feminist of the best kind! He is devoted to justice and equality for women! I love that He raises women up to a place of honour and righteousness and peace!

I am a breakfast lady. I will not even begin to think about the day ahead without my customary bowl of porridge with fruit and Greek yogurt, and a good coffee. It's essential. Equally essential for me is time spent with God at the start of each day. Even, especially, when life is packed full. (I try not to use the word 'busy.' 'Full' is better for me! It's somehow less busy!). I have heard so many women speak about how they don't have time to read their bibles each morning, or they don't know what to read, or they read and then don't understand it or know how to live it. And my heart longs for them to know the satisfying pleasure that comes from the pearly nuggets found in scripture, particularly from Jesus' encounters with women.

Hence *Pearls for Breakfast*. Thoughts to stimulate and nourish, that can be read over breakfast.

My prayer for you as you read these twelve short thoughts is that you will meet with the Saviour in a new way, a helpful way, and a challenging way. Or maybe even for the first time! My prayer is that you will live a life transformed by the power of the Holy Spirit, and that you will know intimacy with the Father like never before.

Blessing you all!

Lynn Lewis

Elizabeth

'After these days his wife Elizabeth conceived, and for five months she kept herself hidden, saying, "Thus the Lord has done for me in the days when he looked on me, to take away my reproach among people."'

Luke 1:24-25.

We meet this older lady, childless and past child-bearing years, early on in Luke's gospel. She was righteous and walked blamelessly; she was without bitterness, despite her shame.

How did she manage this?

Perhaps it was her godly heritage that kept her faithful and loyal to the Lord Almighty.

Maybe she worshipped along with Habakkuk:

*'Though the fig tree should not blossom,
nor fruit be on the vines,
the produce of the olive fail
and the fields yield no food,
the flock be cut off from the fold
and there be no herd in the stalls,*

*yet I will rejoice in the LORD;
I will take joy in the God of my salvation.'*
Habakkuk 3:17-18.

Worship lifts our focus to the One who has the perfect plan for our lives, to the One who is perfect in every way, and to the One who is perfect love.

And then, unexpectedly, suddenly, she was chosen by God to birth the One who would make straight the way for the Lord, and who would be filled with the Holy Spirit even in the womb; the One who would turn the hearts of the fathers, and would go in the spirit and power of Elijah, to make the people ready for the Lord. The Lord anointed Elizabeth to carry this child. He set her apart, having heard the unspoken longing of her heart. He blessed her with more than a child. He blessed her beyond her wildest imaginings to bring John, the Baptiser, into the world. John, who would herald the coming Messiah!

Are you hearing the silence of heaven? Have you been waiting for God to fulfil the longing of your heart? Are you doubting that your prayers are being heard, let alone answered?

Fix your eyes on Jesus, the Author and Perfecter of your faith, the One who sees you, and knows your deepest desires. Gaze at Him. He is good. He is always good, even in the darkness, and even in the depths of despair. There is treasure that can only be found in the depths. There is treasure in the darkness that will only be found in this life. Trust Him, even when you don't understand Him.

Be encouraged by the story of Elizabeth. Commit the longings of your heart to Jesus. Leave your loved ones in the Father's safe, strong hands. Stand under the shadow of His wing. He is good and He is trustworthy.

Jesus, Light of the World, we thank You for the darkness where treasure lies. You own the darkness. Open our eyes that we might see You in all Your splendid glory. We believe that we will see the goodness of God in the land of the living. We look to You. We trust You. Amen.

Anna

'And there was a prophetess, Anna, the daughter of Phanuel, of the tribe of Asher. She was advanced in years, having lived with her husband seven years from when she was a virgin, and then as a widow until she was eighty-four. She did not depart from the temple, worshipping with fasting and prayer night and day. And coming up at that very hour she began to give thanks to God and to speak of him to all who were waiting for the redemption of Jerusalem.'
Luke 2:36-38.

We love Anna, don't we! Like Elizabeth, Anna was childless, faithful and loyal; she was devoted to the Living God, and she was expectant! She was waiting for the redemption of Israel. And so she fasted, she prayed, she worshipped, she prophesied, and she did not depart from the temple. This is amazing, and such an encouragement to us to keep on keeping on. We keep on praying because one day, the door will open. We worship, because we know that worship changes our perspective from natural to supernatural, from ourselves to Jesus. And we operate in the gifts of the Spirit because we know that this brings the kingdom to earth.

But more amazing for us is that there has been a wonderful reversal of who dwells where! We have *become* the temple for the Holy Spirit of God. We host the Spirit of the Lord

God Almighty in our bodies. He tabernacles in us. He dwells in us. We carry the Presence. And we live every part of our lives in the Presence.

Let that glorious truth settle in your heart for a moment.

This is so uplifting! May we be aware of the Presence of God in us. May we host Him well. May He be prominent in us. May we change the atmosphere of the places we visit because God dwells in us, and He is the bringer of life and hope and joy and gladness.

Holy Spirit of the Living God. We thank You that You choose to dwell in us. May we host You well. May we align ourselves with You as we walk through today. May we worship and pray, may we grow the kingdom as we wait for the Saviour to return. Amen.

Martha

'Now as they went on their way, Jesus entered a village. And a woman named Martha welcomed him into her house. And she had a sister called Mary, who sat at the Lord's feet and listened to his teaching. But Martha was distracted with much serving. And she went up to him and said, "Lord, do you not care that my sister has left me to serve alone? Tell her then to help me." But the Lord answered her, "Martha, Martha, you are anxious and troubled about many things, but one thing is necessary. Mary has chosen the good portion, which will not be taken away from her."'
Luke 10:38-42.

There are seven people in scripture whose names are called twice by God. Six of those people are men: Abraham, Jacob, Moses, Samuel, Simon, and Saul. When God calls a name twice, we see Him setting that person apart, and elevating them to a position of favour and honour and responsibility – leader, prophet, priest, evangelist.

So what about the one woman? Martha. She was simply a woman who welcomed Jesus into her home, and became distracted by her cultural mission of providing food and serving well. Isn't it such an encouragement then, that Jesus calls Martha, Martha, at the time when she is anxious, troubled, and distracted? Isn't it an encouragement that

Martha is about to be elevated, even when she's got herself in a state of resentment and petulance?

Even our most ungodly, sinful moments can become holy moments with Jesus. Just as it was for Martha.

We don't know exactly what Jesus has in mind for Martha, but we know that when He next meets her, when Lazarus has died, Jesus reveals to her that He is the Resurrection and the Life. Isn't this Jesus elevating Martha, and affirming her as she affirms that she believes He is the Christ, the Son of God, who is coming into the world?

What a woman of faith! Even in her time of grief. What an ambassador for Christ! Maybe that was her elevation? Maybe. And what a Saviour! Jesus blesses Martha with this revelation at exactly the right moment; the moment when she needs to hear it most.

There must have been a beautiful realisation in Martha's heart, confirmed by the raising of Lazarus. Wonderful!

We can be easily distracted from kingdom matters; there is so much other stuff to do. What are you being distracted by right now? Bring it to Jesus, and leave it in His careful hands. Surrender it to Him. Then listen for Him speaking your name. What is He saying to you today?

Lord Jesus, thank You that You are patient and generous and kind. Forgive me for being easily distracted. Pierce my ears today that I might hear Your voice calling my name. I am listening, Jesus. Amen.

The Freed Woman

'Now he was teaching in one of the synagogues on the Sabbath. And behold, there was a woman who had had a disabling spirit for eighteen years. She was bent over and could not fully straighten herself. When Jesus saw her, he called her over and said to her, "Woman, you are freed from your disability." And he laid his hands on her, and immediately she was made straight, and she glorified God.'
Luke 13:10-13.

For eighteen years, the woman with a disabling spirit lived in the clutches of the enemy. A spirit from hell limited her vision and her movement which would have impacted all other aspects of her life. But not to the point of keeping her away from the synagogue.

And on this particular Sabbath, as ordinary as all the other Sabbaths as far as we can tell, this woman's life was changed by an encounter with Jesus. We don't know her name, but Jesus saw her, He called her, He spoke to her, and He set her free from her disability. She was released from the grip of limitation, and pain, and shame. Her life was transformed, and she glorified God!

Do you need Jesus to see you? Do you need Him to call you? Do you need Him to speak to you? Do you need Him to set you free? Do you need transformation in your life?

Beloved, He sees you. He calls you by name. He speaks forgiveness and life over you. By His stripes you are healed, and in His name, you are set free. No power of hell is too great for Him. No sin is too bad for Him. No pain is too much for Him. No prison is too strong for Him. He is the Lamb who was slain for your sin, and resurrected to glorious life, that you might know His freedom, His grace, His power, His truth and His goodness; in other words, His glory.

He sees you today. He calls you today. Come to Him. Sit with Him. Wait for Him. Listen to Him. Let Him set you free. Let Him raise you up. Let Him honour you.

Jesus, thank You that You see me; You call me; You speak words of freedom and power and tenderness over me. May I encounter You today, may I hear Your voice and know Your touch, that I might be an oak of righteousness for the display of Your splendour in every area of my life. May I be free from the oppression of the enemy. Amen.

The Healed Woman

'As Jesus went, the people pressed around him. And there was a woman who had had a discharge of blood for twelve years, and though she had spent all her living on physicians, she could not be healed by anyone. She came up behind him and touched the fringe of his garment, and immediately her discharge of blood ceased. And Jesus said, "Who was it that touched me?" When all denied it, Peter said, "Master, the crowds surround you and are pressing in on you!" But Jesus said, "Someone touched me, for I perceive that power has gone out from me." And when the woman saw that she was not hidden, she came trembling, and falling down before him declared in the presence of all the people why she had touched him, and how she had been immediately healed. And he said to her, "Daughter, your faith has made you well; go in peace."'

Luke 8:42b-48.

Here is another woman whose name we don't know. We know that she had bled for twelve long years. She must have lived with pain, as well as the shame of being unclean. She had endured the indignity of physical examinations, all for nothing, for no physician had been able to heal her. And yet they had taken her money. We imagine that she would have not felt any physical touch for those twelve long years. We imagine that she would have been lonely. We imagine that she was desperate. We imagine that she knew the scriptures.

She would have known the scriptures about the coming Messiah. She would have heard about Him. He was the One Isaiah prophesied about:

'Instead of your shame there shall be a double portion; instead of dishonour they shall rejoice in their lot; therefore, in their land they shall possess a double portion; they shall have everlasting joy.'

Isaiah 61:7.

Maybe Jesus was the Messiah. And so this woman pursued Jesus despite the crowds. She pursued Jesus despite the fact that she was unclean. She pursued Jesus despite the reality that her life was not in alignment with blessing and favour.

In her desperation, she came from behind, reached for, and touched Jesus. In an instant, her twelve years of misery, and shame, and pain are healed by the One who loved her, and called her His daughter. That is the double portion! That is the joy!

Are you living with pain? Are you living with an unresolved past that keeps you bound in a place of dishonour?

Come to Jesus today. Pursue Him today. Reach out and touch Him today. He does not flinch or turn away. He does not despise. He does not ridicule or mock. No. Instead, He turns. He heals. He affirms. He loves perfectly.

He longs to do this for you.

Jesus, Jehovah-Rapha. Praise You that You are the God who has compassion. Praise You that You are the God who brings healing to my past, and hope for my future. Praise

You that You are the God who calls me daughter. I am Your beloved and You are mine. Amen.

The Well Woman

'A woman from Samaria came to draw water. Jesus said to her, "Give me a drink." (For his disciples had gone away into the city to buy food.) The Samaritan woman said to him, "How is it that you, a Jew, ask for a drink from me, a woman of Samaria?" (For Jews have no dealings with Samaritans.) Jesus answered her, "If you knew the gift of God, and who it is that is saying to you, 'Give me a drink,' you would have asked him, and he would have given you living water." The woman said to him, "Sir, you have nothing to draw water with, and the well is deep. Where do you get that living water? Are you greater than our father Jacob? He gave us the well and drank from it himself, as did his sons and his livestock." Jesus said to her, "Everyone who drinks of this water will be thirsty again, but whoever drinks of the water that I will give him will never be thirsty again. The water that I will give him will become in him a spring of water welling up to eternal life." The woman said to him, "Sir, give me this water, so that I will not be thirsty or have to come here to draw water."'

John 4:7-15.

Jesus had sent His disciples off to find lunch because He was on a mission to rescue, restore, and raise up one particular woman.

The Samaritan woman was desperate, but maybe she wouldn't admit it. She had been cast aside by five husbands. There was no suggestion that she left them. Indeed, under Jewish law, she was not allowed to leave her husband. Only a husband could leave a wife. There was no suggestion of her being an adulteress. Maybe she burned the bread - that was grounds for divorce in the first century BC. She had lived a life of humiliation and shame. She was ostracised - why else would she collect water in the heat of the day?

And it was here at Jacob's well that she found herself talking with a Jewish man about never being thirsty again, and theology, and worship.

She is not the first woman we read about in scripture to meet a man at a well. Abraham's servant, on a mission to find a wife for Isaac, met Rebekah at a well. Jacob met Rachel, who became his wife, at a well. And Moses met Zipporah, who became his wife, at a well.

What if this meeting at Jacob's well was also a betrothal meeting? What if this meeting was about Jesus rescuing this woman from her shame, restoring this woman's dignity, and raising her up to a place of honour because He was about to make her His Bride. He was going to welcome her into the Body of Christ, to be prepared as His Bride?

How awesome is He?

Do you need Him to do this for you? Do you need Him to raise you up to a place of honour and dignity? There is nothing too undignified or too dishonourable for Him.

Do you need Him to restore your value and worth? Do you need to know that He honours you, because you are His Bride?

Let the beauty of those truths take root in your heart today.

Jesus, You are awesome! You are kind! You are tender and merciful, and You are for me. May the truth of the fact that I am honoured and valued in Your sight, precious and dignified, settle in my heart. Thank You, Jesus. I worship You. Amen.

Mary, Martha's Sister

'And [Martha] had a sister called Mary, who sat at the Lord's feet and listened to his teaching.'
Luke 10:39.

'Now when Mary came to where Jesus was and saw him, she fell at his feet, saying to him, "Lord, if you had been here, my brother would not have died." When Jesus saw her weeping, and the Jews who had come with her also weeping, he was deeply moved in his spirit and greatly troubled. And he said, "Where have you laid him?" They said to him, "Lord, come and see."'
John 11:32-34.

'Mary therefore took a pound of expensive ointment made from pure nard, and anointed the feet of Jesus and wiped his feet with her hair. The house was filled with the fragrance of the perfume.'
John 12:3.

This is one lady who loved Jesus very much! She knew how to worship, and she knew how to live from the secret place.

Each time we read about Mary in scripture, she was at the Lord's feet. When Jesus came to her house, she soaked up His teaching. When Lazarus died, she fell at His feet in surrender. And at the supper, she poured out her best worship.

When we sit at the feet of Jesus, when we soak Him in, we will be taken deeper into the Father's heart, and we will dwell (remain, abide) in that secret place. We will live our ordinary lives from that secret place, and we will build the kingdom from that secret place.

Whatever happens in life, we will not be shaken, and we will worship, because we will know the Father's good, good heart, and His peace.

Take a moment to pause today, to be aware of His Presence in the secret place. Sit at the feet of your Saviour, and breathe Him in, slowly and deeply. Release your cares and your burdens. And let the Spirit lead you in worship - make it up! Hum! Sing! Whisper! Dance!

Praise You, Jesus, that You are my secret place. Thank You, Father, for drawing me to Your heart. Thank You that there is a place for me. Let me hear Your heartbeat today, that I may live in alignment with You. Amen.

The Woman Who Worshipped

'*One of the Pharisees asked him to eat with him, and he went into the Pharisee's house and reclined at table. And behold, a woman of the city, who was a sinner, when she learned that he was reclining at table in the Pharisee's house, brought an alabaster flask of ointment, and standing behind him at his feet, weeping, she began to wet his feet with her tears and wiped them with the hair of her head and kissed his feet and anointed them with the ointment. Now when the Pharisee who had invited him saw this, he said to himself, "If this man were a prophet, he would have known who and what sort of woman this is who is touching him, for she is a sinner." And Jesus answering said to him, "Simon, I have something to say to you." And he answered, "Say it, Teacher."*

"A certain moneylender had two debtors. One owed five hundred denarii, and the other fifty. When they could not pay, he cancelled the debt of both. Now which of them will love him more?" Simon answered, "The one, I suppose, for whom he cancelled the larger debt." And he said to him, "You have judged rightly." Then turning toward the woman he said to Simon, "Do you see this woman? I entered your house; you gave me no water for my feet, but she has wet my feet with her tears and wiped them with her hair. You gave me no kiss, but from the time I came in she has not ceased to kiss my feet. You did not anoint my head with oil, but she has anointed my feet with ointment. Therefore I tell you, her

sins, which are many, are forgiven—for she loved much. But he who is forgiven little, loves little." And he said to her, "Your sins are forgiven." Then those who were at table with him began to say among themselves, "Who is this, who even forgives sins?" And he said to the woman, "Your faith has saved you; go in peace."'

Luke 7:36-50.

There is so much going on in this passage. The woman of the city (we don't know her name. I am certain that she was not Mary Magdalene), anointed Jesus' feet as a sign of her worship. She wet His feet with her tears, as a sign of her gratitude. She wiped His feet with her hair, as a sign of her vulnerability. And she kissed His feet, as a sign of her great love for Him. She honoured Jesus wonderfully. How beautiful was that?

And Jesus honoured her. I love how He turned to the woman as He answered Simon. *'Do you see this woman?'* Simon had seen the woman but not in the same way that Jesus. Jesus had seen her worship, her tears, her gratitude, her vulnerability, her love, and her great faith. And He loved her completely.

Do you need to know that Jesus sees you today? He sees you! And He loves you completely. Bask in the beauty of His love today. Let Him honour you. Let Him bless you. Let Him forgive you.

Jesus, You are wonderful. Thank You for Your forgiveness, Your peace, Your grace, Your great, great love, and thank You for the fact that You see me today. Praise Your Holy Name. Amen.

The Women Disciples

'Soon afterward he went on through cities and villages, proclaiming and bringing the good news of the kingdom of God. And the twelve were with him, and also some women who had been healed of evil spirits and infirmities: Mary, called Magdalene, from whom seven demons had gone out, and Joanna, the wife of Chuza, Herod's household manager, and Susanna, and many others, who provided for them out of their means.'

Luke 8:1-3.

When we think of the word minister, we might think of a minister - somebody who is an ordained minister, whose job to do the work of God. Or we might think of the time in a meeting or conference when prayer is offered. Or we might think that somebody has a ministry for those who are sick, or among the homeless. Or somebody might have the gift of ministering prophetically.

These women put a different light on the word minister. They ministered to Jesus as He carried out His ministry. Which means they supported Him. And I think this means that He needed them to do this!

This is such an awesome, humbling privilege, isn't it? To minister to the Living God because He needs you to do this. Think about that.

In the fullness of life, maybe withdraw to the secret place, get with the Holy Spirit, and ask Him, 'How can I minister to You? What can I do that builds the kingdom, and brings glory and honour and fame to Jesus. What do You need me to do?'

Oh Jesus, I bless You, and thank You, that You let me work with You and for You. What a privilege! May I minister well to You today. Show me how I can bless You, the Living God! Amen.

The Forgiven Woman

'The scribes and the Pharisees brought a woman who had been caught in adultery, and placing her in the midst they said to him, "Teacher, this woman has been caught in the act of adultery. Now in the Law, Moses commanded us to stone such women. So what do you say?" This they said to test him, that they might have some charge to bring against him. Jesus bent down and wrote with his finger on the ground. And as they continued to ask him, he stood up and said to them, "Let him who is without sin among you be the first to throw a stone at her." And once more he bent down and wrote on the ground. But when they heard it, they went away one by one, beginning with the older ones, and Jesus was left alone with the woman standing before him. Jesus stood up and said to her, "Woman, where are they? Has no one condemned you?" She said, "No one, Lord." And Jesus said, "Neither do I condemn you; go, and from now on sin no more."'

John 8:1-11.

This situation isn't even really about the woman, or the adultery. It's about Jesus and the Law. But to every woman who has ever lived with shame and humiliation and condemnation, Jesus says, 'Neither do I condemn you; go, and from now on sin no more.'

'Therefore, there is no condemnation for those who are in Christ Jesus.'

Romans 8:1.

Let the truth of this verse settle deep in your heart today. There is no condemnation. There is only freedom, and life in all its fullness, and peace. For every person who ever needed it. All because of the grace of Jesus.

Whatever lies the enemy whispers to you, block them with the truth of scripture: *'There is no condemnation for those who are in Christ Jesus.'*

Whatever guilt the enemy tries to lay on, stand on the truth: *'There is no condemnation for those who are in Christ Jesus.'*

Whatever shame or humiliation the enemy tries to hit you with, refuse to accept it: *'There is no condemnation for those who are in Christ Jesus.'*

This woman's story, which was almost not included in scripture, is there to encourage, and bless, and strengthen those who are familiar with sin and shame. It is a glorious account of the grace of God. Because that's what Jesus is all about. The grace of God. The goodness of God. The generosity of God. All for you.

Jesus. You are amazing. Praise You, and bless You for Your awesome gift of grace. Praise You for Your great love for me. Thank You that there is no condemnation because of the Blood of Jesus. Amen.

Mary Magdalene

'Now when he rose early on the first day of the week, he appeared first to Mary Magdalene, from whom he had cast out seven demons. She went and told those who had been with him, as they mourned and wept. But when they heard that he was alive and had been seen by her, they would not believe it.'

Mark 16:9-11.

Who doesn't love Mary Magdalene?

This woman from whom seven demons were driven out, who was a faithful disciple of Jesus throughout His earthly ministry, who followed Him to the cross, and who went to care for His body at His death, has so many things to teach us. Who doesn't want to sit next to her at the heavenly banquet?

She was an amazing woman of faith. Jesus was bedrock in her life, and she was totally devoted to Him. And it was Mary that He choose to first reveal Himself after His resurrection. What an honour and a privilege for her!

But when she told the others that He was alive, they didn't believe her.

I wonder if this shook her faith? Did she doubt that she had really seen Him, even for a second? Or was she so certain about what she had seen and heard, that there was no doubt in her heart?

In that encounter in the garden with the risen Jesus, did everything He'd said, everything He'd taught, settle into place? Did it glide into place in her heart, or was there an unscrambling of all the puzzling things He'd said, that now fit together and made sense?

It doesn't really matter how it happened. The point is, all that she knew about Jesus, all that she had seen and heard Him teach and do, had been the foundation of her faith, and this encounter irrevocably confirmed the truth of all that He had said, and of all that she knew about Him. She trusted Him and believed Him, even when the eleven didn't trust or believe her.

Sometimes, often, life is not all we would love it to be. There is tension and disappointment, and even grief and sadness.

If you find yourself in this place today, come to Jesus, and hear the tender words He spoke first to Mary, *'Woman, why are you weeping? Whom are you seeking?' (John 20:15)*.

Maybe spend some time in the secret place, declaring all that scripture says God is. Maybe start with Psalm 145. List all the glorious attributes of Father God. Bring your situation to Him, and let His glory cover it.

Father, thank You that You are who You say You are. Thank You that You are trustworthy and true. I commit myself, and my situation, into Your careful hands today, knowing that in Your hands, there is refuge, and safety, and hope. Bless You and praise You, Father God. Amen.

Mary, The Mother of Jesus

'In those days Mary arose and went with haste into the hill country, to a town in Judah, and she entered the house of Zechariah and greeted Elizabeth. And when Elizabeth heard the greeting of Mary, the baby leaped in her womb. And Elizabeth was filled with the Holy Spirit, and she exclaimed with a loud cry, "Blessed are you among women, and blessed is the fruit of your womb! And why is this granted to me that the mother of my Lord should come to me? For behold, when the sound of your greeting came to my ears, the baby in my womb leaped for joy. And blessed is she who believed that there would be a fulfilment of what was spoken to her from the Lord."'

Luke 1:39-45.

Mary, the mother of Jesus was one kingdom woman! And she teaches us three really excellent things in these verses.

First, Mary got up and went.

Do we not also need to get up and go and do what Jesus commanded us to do? He told us to go and preach the gospel. This is simply telling folks that God loves them. He told us to heal the sick. This means praying with those who need prayer for healing. We pray; God does the healing. Jesus told us to drive out demons. We do this with the authority of Jesus; He brings the release. And we are told to raise the dead. This is a bit more of a challenge, but if we broaden our vision, does it not also include dead relationships, dead hopes, dead dreams? This is all kingdom stuff, which we are all commanded to do.

Will you ask Jesus to bring kingdom building opportunities your way this week?

Second, Mary went with haste. There is so much urgency in our lives, in so many ways but is there the same urgency to our kingdom building?

'The harvest is plentiful, but the labourers are few.'
Matthew 9:37.

Will you labour for the kingdom today, this coming month, this year?

Third, Mary carried the Presence of God well, and prominently. Imagine what would happen if folks were filled with the Holy Spirit and prompted to prophesy when they encounter us! That's exactly what happened with Elizabeth when she heard Mary's 'Hi! I'm here!' We read that she was filled with the Holy Spirit, and then we read her prophecy! Amazing!

We all carry the Holy Spirit; He dwells in us. But is He prominent in us? Do we align ourselves with Him so that when we enter a room, or a shop, or an office, the atmosphere is changed?

Will you allow Him to put you on like a glove, so that heaven comes to earth through you? Will you choose to carry Him prominently?

In the fullness of life, maybe make some time to ponder these questions with the Holy Spirit.

Lord Jesus, thank You for the gift of Your Holy Spirit. Holy Spirit, thank You that You are the Presence of God in me, empowering me to build Your kingdom. King of kings, come and be glorified in my life. Fill me again. I surrender my life to You, for Your glory and fame. Amen.

Acknowledgements

My love and thanks to some of the wonderful women in my life…

Alison. Champion of me. Thank you, my darling sister.

Amy. You edited, and read, and suggested, way beyond the call of daughter duty! Thank you, Chick!

Bev. You supported me tirelessly, and endlessly, with complete grace. Thank you.

Dream Team: Lindy and Sally. Aaron and Hur to my Moses! Thank you, both.

The Well Women: Bonny, Cath, Christine, Elaine, Eluned, Ilze, Jayne, Lee, Lindsay, and Llinos. This wouldn't have happened without you all! Thank you for your prayers, your love, and your encouragement!

Printed in Great Britain
by Amazon